Dealing with Aggressive Debt Collectors
What to do and how to do it by an industry insider

By Michelle Dunn

Table of Contents

Foreword

When bill collectors start calling my first reaction is to cringe away from the phone. It seems so much easier to ignore the problem and hope it, along with the calls, and my debt, goes away. Of course we all know this will never happen and so we do have to deal with it. I wrote this book based on my experience as a debtor and a collector. I am hoping that by being on both sides of the fence my story can help you deal with collectors who break the law – and those who don't, can help you learn how to get out of debt and give you the tools and resources you need to deal with collectors, clear up your debt and move on with your life.

Being in debt is very stressful and normally people go into debt when they are already over stressed – for me it was during a divorce which was almost too much to handle, and then I not only had to deal with getting a divorce, but working full time with two kids, not receiving child support or help with the children, balancing the house, pets, kids, jobs, bills and divorce proceedings all while being an emotional mess and having to talk to bill collectors because I no longer made enough money to pay my bills.

If you are reading this book I am sure you have been there or are there now – and it is not a fun place to be. I hope this book can help you leave that place and help you move forward. This is my personal story, what I did, what steps I took and how I overcame it. I hope it can help you.

Dealing with Aggressive Debt Collectors, What to do and how to do it by an industry insider

Michelle Dunn

Available in paperback and for your Kindle

www.MichelleDunn.com
www.Credit-and-Collections.com

ISBN #: 9781475191387

Dealing with Debt – my story

I found myself in debt when I was getting a divorce and suddenly found myself having to learn everything I could about dealing with debt, and how to pay it off while still paying living expenses for myself and my two children while having one less income. I was married for 10 years and had two children. When I was getting divorced I was living in the house with the kids and working full time. I felt like things couldn't get any worse with money, since I only had my income and still had to pay for upkeep on the house as well as all the other expenses. I started thinking about which things I could do without to save some money. To start, I cancelled the guy who plowed our driveway and got rid of cable television right away, which made me feel better because now I would have that much more money each month.

I had to get my bills all together so I could look at them and really figure out how much I owed, how much I was going to have to pay out each month and how much I made. I didn't think I would make enough to pay all the bills I had. I put all my bills in a pile. I had a notebook and calculator and a sticky notepad. I added everything up and figured out the totals and I did not make enough to pay everything. I put all the bills that were necessities in a pile, the mortgage payment, electric bill, phone (negotiable, but I live in the woods and had 2 little kids), food, daycare, gas, heat, insurance for house and car. Then I had a pile of bills that were just really my own fault, a car payment, credit cards for department stores and Visa, a payment for a chest freezer we had in our basement. I know these are not negotiable bills but at the time I was an emotional wreck trying to keep it together and paying the bills I thought were the necessities made me at least feel like I was providing enough for my kids and being a good mother. I felt like these other creditors could just take a hike if I couldn't pay. Being in debt is an emotional time and then add divorce and other family problems into it and that is why collectors sometimes have such a hard time getting paid.

My income was not enough to even pay my necessities so in order to be able to pay my necessities and pay the car and credit card bills, I needed to call my phone company and electric company and talk about paying less each month. People don't realize you can do this, I never knew either until I was in a position that I had to ask for their help or live in more of a financial mess. I explained my situation to the phone company, about how my income went from two to one, how I knew I didn't really have to have a phone but I had two small children and would feel more comfortable being able to call for help if I needed it. She explained to me that they could put me on a restricted type plan, where I would not be able to make long distance calls, but could call local and 911 and as long as I sent a very low payment each month and didn't add to my bill, they could do that for 6 months. I was very excited. I felt like I was getting somewhere and digging myself out of a hole.

When I called the electric company they couldn't really give me less electricity but they did set me up on a payment plan and I did walk around in the dark a lot. They also had a program where you could offer some community service in exchange for part of your electric bill. I picked up trash along the highway. I have to tell you when I arrived to pick up the trash and even the time leading up to it I felt terrible and embarrassed that I couldn't make enough money to pay the electric bill so my kids could have power. Once I got there, everyone was really nice and I knew they were in the same situation and we had a good time. Well, as much fun as you can have with a bunch of broke strangers picking up trash on the side of the road.

I called the credit card companies and explained my situation to them. They were not as easy to understand or care about my situation so it took some time on the phone and I had to explain it to them a few times. At one point I explained that if they didn't take a lesser payment, I was putting their bill at the bottom of my pile and calling my other creditors to work out payment plans so they could keep getting something from me while I was having a hard time. Then if there was any money left after that I would call them back to see if they wanted that each month. It worked; she set up a payment plan with me right then on the phone and even cancelled the interest for 6 months to help some of my payment cover the principal. I of course had stopped using the card and cancelled it – you may not have to cancel the card but I didn't want to have a credit card anymore. I felt like it was just adding to my problems – I would rather go without something than buy it on credit.

I now had new payments on all of my bills and it was tight. Sometimes I had to go to the local church food pantry for food because I didn't have enough money left over for groceries. I made my bills for a while but when the furnace broke, and I had to pay a repair bill, and I needed tires for my car and my kids needed shoes – I couldn't make it anymore and had to move out of the house. I just didn't make enough money to live there with the upkeep and my income.
I am happy to say I eventually paid off all my debt, and am currently debt free. My advice: Stand up for yourself and always ask for help when you need it.

What I did:

To break it down into easy steps I want to list exactly what I did because this might work for you as well. Everyone is different and some have more or less debt – but the things I did can be used as guidelines for yourself or just steps to help you get back on track.

- I gathered all my bills together so I could add everything up and figure out what I owed compared to what I made.
- Cancelled credit cards and called them to set up payments and ask for late fees and interest to be held or written off.
- Called everyone I owed money to and set up realistic payment plans that I could commit to. If someone wouldn't work with me, I put them at the bottom of the pile and kept going.
- When I was setting up the payment plans on the credit cards, I tried to pay the most to the cards that charged the highest interest rate so I could pay them off quicker.

Steps to take right now:

What you can do today to help yourself is sit down with a calculator, a notebook, your bills and paystubs. Just add up everything you owe each month and as a total. This way you can see the big picture of what you owe. I had an idea of how much I paid to the electric company, phone company and my other bills but I didn't know collectively how much I was really paying out each month. Here are the steps you can take today:

- Cancel your credit cards – to get out of your situation you have to stop using credit.
- Call everyone you owe money to, explain your situation and set up realistic payments. Stand up for yourself, if someone asks you to pay more than you know you can pay – tell them you would like to but you can't. Don't put yourself in a position where you still can't pay your bills.
- Try to pay off bills that have a higher interest rate first, it will save you money in the long run.

3 most important ways to deal with debt collectors

The biggest mistake you can make when you are in debt or feel that you are sliding into more debt and losing control is to stop communicating with the person or company you owe money to. If you can keep the lines of communication open with your creditor and avoid having the account sent to a third party collection agency, you can avoid having to deal with those collectors at all! Here are the top 3 best ways to deal with a bill collector:

Communicate! Don't ignore the debt – talk to them and explain your situation. They can't help you if you don't communicate. When you don't communicate it sends the message that you either don't care what they do – example – place the account with a collection agency, report it to your credit report, take you to court – or whatever they have to do to get paid. It also makes a creditor mad – they feel as though they have a relationship with you, and when you ignore them, it is a slap in the face. I have been a collector and when a customer doesn't respond – we take action to get the debt paid in a more aggressive manner – BUT if you tell us the problem we may be able to help. It costs money for a business to write off your balance due, they lose all profit, and then they have to pay someone to collect the money for them – they would rather work with you and have you just pay them. That is a win-win for them and you.

Make realistic payment offers. Don't accept a payment plan a collector is pushing on you if you don't intend to make that payment or can't afford that payment. You are only hurting yourself – the collector doesn't care – they can take legal action to get paid. Stand up for yourself – make a realistic payment offer that you can make and if the collector won't accept that hang up. Don't be ridiculous and offer $5 a month on a $5,000.00 debt or you won't be taken seriously.

If you really want to pay off your debt and work with the collector you need to be:
- Realistic
- Firm
- In control
- Educated

Know your rights. If a collector won't agree to your suggested payment – let them know that is all you can do– so they can accept your offer or "do what they have to do". This will cost them more money and time and they might not ever get paid, when they could easily work with you and accept the payment plan even if it is for a limited time. Like the phone company did with me, they offered me help with a time limit – 6 months. Before you talk to a collector learn and know your rights. I tell people that if they are dealing with collectors they need to print out the FDCPA, Fair Debt Collection Practices Act, and know what a collector can and cannot do and what they can and cannot do. You can find the FDCPA at www.FTC.gov

The 5 most important things to remember when dealing with a debt collector:
1. Keep a paper trail
2. Know your rights
3. Act quickly, don't put it off
4. Ask questions
5. Have patience

TRY THIS! Can you increase your income and decrease your expenses? Try canceling your credit cards, cut up your cards and only use your debit card.

REMEMBER:
Money isn't worth losing sleep over
Money isn't worth fighting with your family
Money isn't worth being so stressed you lose your cool and scream and yell
Money isn't worth drinking to forget about it
Money isn't worth Divorce
Money isn't worth breaking the law

Dealing with aggressive collectors on the phone

When I found myself in debt, I had collectors calling me every day, some were nice and others were not. I paid the collectors that were nice to me first, and the collectors that were rude and loud, got paid the smallest amount last. I have found this to be true as a bill collector as well, when I owned my collection agency and would call people, they would tell me they were going to pay me first because I was nice to them. You probably know that when someone owes money to one person, many times they owe to others as well and honey gets more love than hate.

I had one collector that was calling me for the payment on that freezer I had in my basement – even though I had called them when I called all my other creditors, they didn't want to hear it. They wanted to continue receiving the scheduled monthly payment no matter what. I couldn't make that payment, though I continued to send them payment, just less than what was due. They ended up placing the account with a collection agency. There was some time between when they placed it and when I had sent them my last payment where they did not contact me and then once the agency had processed my account, they started calling me. It was the same guy every time and he would call at dinner time. I would rush in from work and picking my kids up at daycare, trying to get them settled and make them dinner and this guy would call. He would say things like:

"If you just got home from work you have a paycheck, why aren't you paying this?"

"You should be a better mother to your children and pay your bills"

"We are going to come and take the freezer" I told them to come get it, it is unplugged and empty and ready to go – this really made the collector mad and he called me a lowlife Bitch. I hung up.

"I know where you work and I am going to call your boss and tell him you aren't paying your bills"

"I will keep calling you every day until you mail a payment" I told him I had been paying every month and the creditor was cashing my checks, this shut him up for only a minute where he said I wasn't meeting my obligations and was a dirt bag. I hung up.

"I know you have kids and I will find out where they go to school"

At this point, since I was going through a divorce and my ex-husbands name was on all of these bills with mine – and the divorce wasn't final I asked my divorce attorney what to do. Since the freezer was the only debt in just my ex-husbands name – I gave the collector his name and where he worked and stopped paying this debt completely. Once my ex-husband got contacted I started getting calls from him as well as the collectors – I quickly learned to shut off the ringer on my phone when I got home.

Some collectors know that people in debt are sometimes in emotional turmoil and they use that information to their advantage – they think that when you are down or feeling down that is the perfect time for them to try and push you around. Don't let this happen to you, stand up for yourself, be strong and if you feel like you might cry, hang up. As long as you are doing the best you can do, no one can bring you down. I refuse to let anyone talk to me in a disrespectful manner and you should do the same.

Many people think collection agencies are out there just trying to make a buck at your expense. A collection agency is a service business just like a dry cleaner. A company hires them when they don't get paid, and expects them to collect and send them the money. When I started my own collection agency I wasn't thinking about how I could squeeze money out of people with no money so that I could have more money. I started my agency because I had worked in accounts receivable and then as a credit manager for many companies and for many years. I started my agency so I could have flexibility in my schedule and be home for my children. Of course I hoped I would make money but it didn't cross my mind to start an agency to make huge amounts of money by harassing people or yelling at them or by breaking the law. I hadn't done that as a credit manager and I didn't do it as an agency owner.

Some agencies do break the law but that represents a small number of agencies. Unfortunately those are the only agencies that are discussed by consumers and the media. Because of the feelings consumers have about debt it is easy to blame or be angry at whoever is asking you to pay. When someone owes you money and you have to visit them or call them for your money, how do you feel? Is it justifiable for the person who owes you the money to be angry at you and yell and swear at you? You did them a favor by allowing them to borrow money from you and now because you want to be paid back, you are the bad guy.

What I did

I want to share some of the responses I used to the above comments made by the collector that you can use as a guide when an aggressive bill collector calls you.

Collector: "If you just got home from work you have a paycheck, why aren't you paying this?"
Me: "Because my income outweighs my debts. If you looked at my file you already know this and must be calling to offer me a settlement or new payment plan."

Collector: "You should be a better mother to your children and pay your bills"
Me: Hang up. That is just abuse, there is no solution here or any way to have a constructive discussion – don't waste your time or breath speaking to a collector who says something like this to you – they are not trying to get the bill paid, they are just trying to make you cry or mad and start a fight – I mean really! Do collectors really think someone is going to say – this collector is awesome he puts me down and is an asshole – let me send him a check!

Collector: "We are going to come and take the freezer"
Me: I told them to come and get it, it is unplugged and empty and ready to go – this really made the collector mad and he called me a lowlife Bitch. I hung up.

Collector: "I know where you work and I am going to call your boss and tell him you aren't paying your bills"
Me: Great! I will get in touch with my attorney since that is a violation of the FDCPA. Hang up.

Collector: "I will keep calling you every day until you mail a payment"
Me: I told him I had been paying every month and the creditor was cashing my checks, this shut him up for only a minute where he said I wasn't meeting my obligations and was a dirt bag. I hung up. At this point don't even bother to contact your creditor – I did and they did not care – they said to just deal with the agency. Creditors who use agencies that abuse debtors are as worthless as the aggressive collector.

Collector: "I know you have kids and I will find out where they go to school and get off the bus"
Me: Hang up – obviously a collector that is disturbed.

What you can do right now

If you are in a position where collectors are calling you – take a minute and visit the Federal Trade Commission website at www.FTC.gov – read and print the FDCPA and keep it by your phone so you are ready for the next call.

Educate yourself on your rights. Know what a bill collector can and cannot do and don't take any bullying from them. Just don't do it – if someone says something inappropriate to you – hang up. If you are so inclined you can also report them to the BBB and any trade associations that agency belongs to. Though keep in mind many aggressive collectors or collectors that break the law are not in good standing with the BBB and don't belong to any associations – which is why they continue to act like this, so that may not do you any good. You can always report it to your Attorney General's office or call 877-FTC-HELP to let the Federal Trade Commission know about your complaint. Otherwise – let it go – don't let their negativity affect you – you are already under enough stress.

If at all possible try to work with your creditors BEFORE your account gets placed with a third party collection agency – they you don't have to deal with them at all!

Don't hide and ignore the debt – communication is key. If you can't pay, talk to them or send a letter, if you get a collection notice and don't know what it is, don't just toss it – write back and ask for verification. I would advice writing to ask for this rather than asking over the phone so that you have a dated paper trail.

Keep that paper trail, pay with checks so you have a record of all payments, take notes when a collector calls, keep a notebook and pen by the phone with the copy of the FDCPA. Mail anything you send to a collector by certified mail or priority mail with delivery confirmation. Be prepared to defend yourself.

If a collector keeps calling you and you keep having to hang up just keep asking for them to send you something in writing and hang up. Sometimes they do and sometimes they don't. In my situation the collector did not send me anything and just kept calling.

If you just can't deal with everything try to work with a reputable debt management company and do your research! I tried working with a company like this called New Horizons and they ripped me off – they said they would call my creditors and work out payment plans and then I would just send them a monthly payment and they would disperse the payments to my creditors. I sent them my checks and they never paid my creditors – talk about digging the hole deeper!

Top 10 mistakes people make when dealing with debt collectors

1. Avoiding calls – when you don't communicate with a collector it only makes the situation worse for you, they might just file suit because they don't know why you aren't responding or if there is a dispute.

2. Over-committing to a payment they cannot afford or make. Just because a collector says you have to pay a certain amount each month doesn't mean that you can. Stay within your means.
3. Telling collectors you sent a payment you didn't – you will always get caught in this lie, just tell them you didn't send it if you didn't send it but be prepared to tell them when you will send it.
4. Feeling intimidated and getting angry. Once you get angry things sometimes get said that shouldn't and there isn't a resolution to the problem. If you feel intimidated say something or tell them you can't talk to them right now and hang up. Stand up for yourself.
5. Ignoring letters. When you ignore the letters from a collection agency and the mail is not returned, they will normally file suit. They don't know why you aren't responding and so assume the debt is valid.
6. Lying. When you tell a collector you don't have a job and that is why you can't pay, don't post about a bad day at work on your Facebook page.
7. Not getting it in writing. Keep a paper trail, you need it to protect yourself. Any payment arrangements, settlement offers or payments or any agreements you make with a collector, get it in writing.
8. Not asking for proof of the debt within the first 30 days of receiving the first collection letter – don't put it off, ask for this right away if you need it.
9. Waiting to long to dispute a debt. You have a certain amount of time by law to dispute a debt, if you wait to long the debt is considered legally valid.
10. Don't write bad checks to a collection agency. It's better not to make a payment than to pay with a bad check.

Dealing with Zombie Debt – what is zombie debt?

Zombie debt is old debt that you thought was dead and buried and keeps coming back to life. Zombie debt may be something new to you or new to the news media right now but it is not anything new. This type of old re-sold debt has been around for years but is only getting public attention right now. Zombie debt varies from state to state because there are different state laws in each state, this debts statute of limitations can also be "re-set" when you make a payment which most consumers do not know. State laws determine the statute of limitations on particular types of debts, and may vary depending on the type of debt and the laws in the state you live in or the state the creditor is in or where the contract was signed. To find out about the statute of limitations on your old debt contact your State Attorney General's Office www.naag.org

Many consumes think that if they let a debt go unpaid for years they never have to pay it and it goes away. Your debt never goes away – if you don't pay it, you still owe it unless you file bankruptcy in some cases. It is not illegal for a collector to try to collect on old debt. The only restriction on time-barred debt is that legal action cannot be taken to try and get paid – but a collector can still try to collect on any debts that are owed legally.

Dealing with collectors of Zombie Debt

If a collector calls you about a debt you feel is 'zombie debt", and you aren't sure if you even owe this debt ask questions. My top 3 questions to ask the collector:

1. How old is this debt? Is it past the statute of limitations?
2. When was my last payment?
3. Send me proof I owe this debt, or verification of the debt.

Once you hang up with a collector and have asked these questions, put it in writing and send it certified mail to the collection agency. If you don't receive verification within 30 days, send another letter stating you had requested this information on a specific date, and did not receive it, you are disputing this debt ask that they stop trying to collect on an invalid claim. By law (FDCPA) collectors that do not send you verification within 30 days cannot legally continue to try and collect on that specific debt. This is where it gets hairy – because they can no longer collect in this instance, they then sell the debt to another agency who will begin contacting you. Unfortunately and as unfair as this is – it is legal and happens every day. So if you can just keep in mind that you may have to do this a few more times in order to get agencies to stop calling you, you will have less frustration. Remember, you might have owed this money at one time and were unable to pay it, or maybe it is not even your debt at all, it could be an identity theft situation BUT you will have to be the one to take the above steps to stop having collectors call you about the debt. Debts can be sold and re-sold many time and this will keep happening until they stop selling it. It is my hope that the FTC will put some new laws in place to deal with these types of unproductive situations.

Paying an old debt is up to you – maybe you already have bad credit and don't care. Maybe you want to make good on your bills and will pay, everyone is different but be prepared no matter which option you choose. Even though you can't be sued on an old debt, you still owe it and bill collectors can continue to try and collect it from you. Not paying a debt you owe, no matter how old it is can make it harder for you or more expensive for you to get credit, insurance, an apartment or a job.

When you make a payment on an old debt that you have not made a payment on in a long time the statute of limitations is revised to begin at the date of the most recent payment. Once that happens you can be sued for this particular debt, it can be put on your credit report if it isn't there already.

If you decide the debt is valid and you want to just pay it off so it will go away, ask for a settlement amount. Many times you can get a settlement offer that is much less than the total amount due. If you do this – get it in writing from the collector. Never send a settlement payment without having something in writing. Without having this in writing this settlement payment can just be applied to the balance due as a payment on your account with the balance due.

What is Credit?

Traditionally, credit is only used so we can live beyond our means or because we are not dedicated enough to save money and will pay someone to satisfy the "I want it now" mentality. Many people have a cavalier attitude towards credit; some feel it is "owed" to them. Credit can fulfill self esteem issues by enabling us to "buy" friends by getting the check, or having 2 tickets for a show. Shopping is the #1 feel better activity when someone is depressed or sad.

Some of the most educated people with great jobs and great paychecks get so far into debt they file for bankruptcy and fall into a depression. Credit problems are not a poor persons problem or a rich persons problem, it's a persons problem, many times stemming from personal issues. No one teaches us about debt, credit or credit cards and how it all works, how it affects us and how it can change our life.

When you mention the word credit the first thing that comes to most people's minds is "bad". Credit means so many things but in this book we are talking about your credit or credit that has been extended to you resulting in debt.

Most credit problems are unexpected. No one gets credit for things with the intention of not paying and just running off into the sunset. Some of the most common causes of credit problems are:

Unexpected medical bills
No savings
No experience dealing with money or a budget
Unemployment
Overextending yourself
Accidents
Separation and divorce
Death of a spouse

Many people use credit to quiet nagging children and so that their kids don't have to go without as they did. Credit is used to keep up with the neighbors and to occupy children's time or baby-sit children so we can do something else. In other words we buy something to act as a babysitter so we don't have to spend time with our children.

Consumers believe that the more credit you have, the more successful you are. For example the platinum card makes us feel special; a gold card means we are better or more successful than our neighbor who only has a silver card. The credit card companies play on our feelings of self esteem and take advantage of those feelings and market to our feelings in order to make as much money off us as possible whether we can afford it or not.

People don't want to live within their means, they want more and they want it now. Using a credit card to fulfill that dream when you can't make ends meet is equivalent to making a deal with the devil. Watch out. We have freedom in America, make the right choice. Educate yourself and your children about debt and credit before it is too late.

What is Debt?

The word debt is another word that makes us cringe but what is debt? Debt is an obligation or promise to pay something on a certain date and by a certain time.

Debt is what you owe people who gave you credit so you could have something now instead of saving up for that item and buying it when you had enough money. Bad debt is what happens when you don't pay your bills. When you don't pay your utility bills, you may have your phone or electricity shut off. Missing a car payment can result in repossession. Missing credit card payments results in a bill the next month that is double your monthly payment plus a late fee. Your credit cards can be "shut off" and/or you can be placed with a collection agency and the late payments will be reflected on your credit report. This can hurt you when you try to rent an apartment or get a job.

It is really to your advantage to make every effort to pay your bills or make payment arrangements if you get in a bind. Business owners all sell products with the understanding that you will pay your bill. If you have problems, don't be embarrassed, contact anyone you owe money to and you will be surprised at how helpful people will be when they see that you want to solve your payment problem instead of ignoring them until they feel as though you are avoiding them and they will not be paid.

Why is America in such debt? The answer is simple, we want it now. We want to keep up with the neighbors, we want to appear more successful than we perceive ourselves to be and we "think" we can catch up on our bills. Business owners everywhere that offer credit, offer this credit so they can make more money by extending credit to customers so that those customers can "afford" their products or services. Business owners then lose money when their customers don't make their payments. Those business owners then get angry when they don't receive your payment or any explanation as to why you have not paid, think of it as "disrespect". Business owners would rather you paid them than having to chase you for their money. With this in mind remember if you can't make a payment the best thing you can do is CALL.

Debt causes us so much stress which affects our relationships, our physical and mental health, and can contribute to depression, anxiety, sleeplessness' and divorce. When we realize we are in over our heads we want to hide it. We are embarrassed, feel ashamed, guilty, mad at ourselves, frustrated, we feel despair and as if we are a failure. Our self esteem plummets and we feel out of control, overwhelmed, unhappy and scared. On top of all that we don't want anyone to know! Therefore we don't let anyone help us or take advice from anyone because we want everyone to think that everything is just fine.

How Credit & Debt affect you

I had good credit until I went through a divorce. Then I had terrible credit. It was awful, here I was a bill collector and I had bill collectors calling me and sending me letters. Unfortunately, I didn't have any money even though I had a full time job. I was barely able to make my mortgage payment, pay my taxes and then support myself and my children. Even more unfortunately, my ex husband didn't feel the need to make child support payments so it was my income to support myself and my two young children for a while.

Since I was already working full time, I had to come up with a plan or I was not going to be able to stay in my house and care for my kids. I took out all my bills and made a list of them, and then I decided what I could cut out so I could have more money to pay the important bills, such as mortgage and gas for my car so I could get to work. Some of the things I got rid of were the cable television, cell phone, any entertainment such as movies or going out. I then called all of the companies that I had a bill with such as the phone company, and the electric company and told them that I was living alone with my children on one salary and that I could not make the full monthly payment that they required and what could I do?

They ALL worked with me and helped me. For example the phone company let me pay approximately $10-$20 a month towards my bill, as long as I didn't make long distance calls or run up my bill. The electric company let me pay a small monthly amount until I could pay more, and told me about going to my town for assistance.

I have to tell you this was one of the most depressing times of my life. Here I was, working a full time job and having to go to the town for help with my electric bill and going to the local church to get food because I just didn't have enough money to go to the grocery store. I spent many nights sitting on the couch crying after I put my kids to bed.

I was determined and motivated and continued studying and learning all I could about my industry so I could ask my boss for a raise, which I did and which I got. That helped me to feel more empowered and I continued to pay my bills as I could and spend time with my children doing free things on the weekends.

Debt Consolidation

If you decide to try and consolidate your debts in order to make one monthly payment, do your research! There are many debt consolidation companies out there that will take your money but not send it to your creditors, look out for these scams! I had this happen to me once and then the company abandoned the building they had been in and disappeared off the face of the earth, with all the money I had been sending them each month. I was now even more in debt, I still owed the creditors who were expecting this company so send them money from me each month and I was out the thousands of dollars I sent to this "debt consolidation" company. Do not let this happen to you!

Some things you can do to verify a company is not a scam job:

- Check references and with the Better Business Bureau
- Check their interest rate and compare that to your banks rate to be sure you are getting the lowest possible rate or the best deal.
- Look for hidden fees.
- Consider a non-profit credit counseling service in your area.

Budgeting

Just what is a budget? Do people really use them?

A budget is your spending plan; it is usually based on your income and your expenses, so everyone's budget is a little different. When you say "budget" people run screaming from the room, but a budget does not have to be scary. Let me share with you how you can create your own monthly budget.

Income: Figure out your monthly take home pay after taxes.
Expenses: List your payments for each month, this will include things like:
Rent or mortgage
Utilities
Credit cards
Auto loans, student loans, personal loans, any loans at all.
Food, eating in and eating out.
Fuel
Insurance
Medical bills

Then add up your total expenses and your total income. Subtract your bills from your earnings. Are you looking at a negative number? If so, go back and cut back on some expenses. If something seems too hard to give up, give it up for one month and try it.
Being in debt is stressful, adjusting to a budget can be tough work in the beginning but the rewards are great. Changing your credit is a lot like dieting, it seems like you take all these steps and when you look down, you're still flabby. Keep at it, it takes some time and really does work. You will lessen the stress in your life causing yourself to be much more relaxed and happier and allowing the people around you to enjoy your company again!

TRY THIS!

For the next month, keep a record of every penny you spend. At the end of the month, compare the total you spent with how much you have earned. When you see what you spend your money on, it is easier to take control of your spending!

Repairing your Credit

The first thing you want to do is create a budget, see the end of this book for a worksheet you can use. This will be part of your Credit Plan.

You're Credit Plan

- Make a list of your debts and bills and include the total balance and monthly payment amount.
- Take your credit cards out of your wallet and stop using them.
- Arrange your debt in order of the largest interest charges.
- Call each credit card company and tell them your situation. Cancel the cards you don't need, or all of them if you can! Set up re-payment plans with the credit card companies.
- While you pay off the biggest interest charged cards pay the minimum amount due on all your bills each month.
- Starting with your highest interest rate credit cards or bills, pay an additional $100 or whatever your total savings per month is from: Carpooling
  Bringing lunch from home
  Bringing coffee from home
  Not buying movies or magazines
  Money saved from canceling cable or cell phones

Your Credit Responsibilities

Once you are approved and take out a loan, make all your payments on time. If your payment is late, you can be charged a late fee. Your late payment may also be reflected on your credit report.

If you find yourself in a situation where you are going to be late with a payment, the best thing to do is to contact that creditor IMMEDIATELY. I cannot stress this enough. Most creditors will try to work with you if they can. If you miss a couple or a few payments, especially without any communication, your creditor may place you with a collection agency, revoke your credit, report your delinquency to the credit bureaus, begin foreclosure or repossess the item or items. Many honest and hardworking people are losing their homes due to foreclosures. The first step to avoid this is to act on the problem as soon as you realize you have a problem. Make a plan NOW because later is too late.

Stopping the Cycle of bad credit and bad debt is up to you. Education about credit and debt needs to start with our children. According to "Born to Buy" author Juliet B. Schor, kids can recognize logos by 18 months old. By ages 6 and 7 girls are asking for the latest fashions and the average 8-13 year old is watching over 3 ½ hours of television a day. American children watch approximately 40,000 commercials in one year, making about 3,000 requests for "stuff" that they see advertised each year.

Every child wants to fit in, or be cool and parents sometimes who work a lot of hours or who are not home will substitute money for their time. So they buy (charge on their credit card) their kids the latest $85 sneakers, to alleviate their guilt and make their child happy, or so they think. Being a child who never had the "cool" clothes or sneakers in the 70's and 80's, I know how important these "things" can be. I had to baby-sit, rake leaves, wash cars, shovel snow, and do errands or whatever I could come up with to have any money to buy things that I wanted but that my mother said I didn't "need". This is a great lesson but something most kids aren't learning. My parents never had a credit card, if we didn't have the money for it, we didn't have it. When I was a kid I thought this was cruel and unjust punishment but now I see that this taught me a lot about working, and making my own money, and then how I wanted to spend that money that was sometimes hard to earn. It taught me about saving up for something I wanted and I would always be trying to come up with new ways to make more money.

Some parents don't want their children to "suffer" like they did and think they will give their kids everything they didn't have, give them a better life. When you do this, you are doing a disservice to your children, to yourself and to the people your children have to deal with. You are setting up your children for failure.

You won't always be there (or shouldn't be) to buy your children what they want, though you will always provide them with what they "need". I have friends who have spoiled their children, cell phones, clothes from the mall, cars, laptops, anything they want. One woman I know has a daughter who moved out of the house but is struggling with her checkbook. Her parent's pay her rent, electric bill, drop off groceries and let her come to their house every weekend to do her laundry and pick up more food. They pay her cell phone bill, bought her a car and laptop "for school" and never taught her how to handle money or use a checkbook. She has no idea what a budget is and she can't balance her checkbook. Fortunately for her, that is okay, she doesn't have to know how to do all these things because her mom continues to do them for her. When she bounces a check, she calls her mom who deposits enough to cover the bad check and a little extra so her daughter can go out with friends. Instead of showing her how to handle her money and be successful the parents are enabling this poor girl in such a way that she can never be successful unless they stop bailing her out.

Giving and giving, more and more to our children doesn't help them. You are seriously impairing their ability to be a productive and successful adult. Kids may like getting all this "stuff" from their parents but imagine how they feel when they get older and can be independent and proud.

Good credit is something that is earned, you teach this to your children just like good eating habits or study habits. How can you expect healthy children if you don't eat right, teach them about nutrition and eating right by setting an example.

As parents it is our job to educate our children about money, credit and debt, health, the importance of education, and offset the damage done by the commercialization of childhood in our society.

When I had my own children and they were in grade school, my business took off. I was doing well and credit card offers started coming in the mail. I was so excited! I filled them out and started receiving credit cards in the mail. In my mind money equaled success and I couldn't have been more wrong.

We become addicted to credit cards because when we use them and don't pay off the balance each month they become a necessity to live. When our income changes or our marital status changes we use the credit cards to live. I was charging gas, groceries, games and clothes for my kids, anything we wanted. I justified this by telling myself I must be doing great or these credit card companies wouldn't have sent me a credit card with such a high limit! WRONG!

Once you can't make the payments and the cards are shut off, you go from extreme happiness to sadness, depression, low self esteem, feeling overwhelmed, embarrassed and like a failure. You try to act like everything is great but you're a sinking ship and won't ask for help. Just like everyone else who finds themselves in this situation I wanted to maintain that I was successful and worthy, and so I hid the shame of my debt and suffered while everyone who had to deal with me suffered as well.

3 steps to eliminate debt:

1. Stop going into debt
2. Spend less than you make
3. Pay off debt with the difference between 1 & 2

While you deal with collectors and your debt, you can feel frustrated, upset, angry, embarrassed and a whole slew of other emotions. Keep in mind that you are not alone – the Total U.S. consumer debt was $2.43 trillion, as of May 2011 (Source: Federal Reserve's G.19 report on consumer credit, released July 2011). So how many Americans are in debt? Excluding minors, the total is somewhere in the neighborhood of 80% if we include secured debts like homes and cars. Excluding those particular purchases puts us closer to 50% of the adult population, and half of that 50% has thousands of dollars owed. (Source: http://www.americandebtadvisor.com/)

Every American's credit report has been affected by the recession, so you are clearly not alone. But you are one of the few who is taking control of your situation and removing debt from your life so you are already ahead of the game in this new economy.

The laws – Fair Debt Collection Practices

The FDCPA is a federal statute and many states have collection laws that are very similar or the same. Keep in mind that this act was not written for debt collectors but for consumers in response to outrage by debtors about abusive collection actions during the 70's. This act helps to provide a defense against third party debt collectors. First party debt collectors, or original creditors, do not have to follow the Fair Debt Collection Practices Act.

According to the Better Business Bureau, debt collectors resolve 85% of the complaints received against them, which is significantly higher than any other industry.

Only the collection of consumer debts are covered and regulated by the FDCPA. Business debts are NOT covered by the FDCPA. The FDCPA covers:

Personal debts
Family debts
Household debts
Some examples would be:
Personal credit card accounts
Auto loans
Medical bills
A mortgage

A debt collector under the FDCPA is any person who uses mail, the internet, or the telephone for the principal purpose of collecting a debt. In other words, a person who's job is collecting past due debts. This also includes anyone who regularly attempts to collect debts owed to someone other than themselves. There are exceptions to this, for example, the term debt collector under the FDCPA includes any original creditor who is trying to collect their own debt and is using a different name which indicates a third party is trying to collect. This can include lawyers, law firms, landlords or home owner associations.

Most Common FDCPA Violations:

- Contacting consumers at inconvenient times
- Making repetitive phone calls
- Harassment and verbal abuse
- Threatening to harm one's person or reputation
- Contacting a consumer when the debt collector knows the consumer is represented by an attorney
- Contacting a consumer if the debt collector knows the debt is disputed and the consumer has requested verification of the debt
- Not verifying information and contacting the wrong person

The FDCPA imposes restrictions on various practices for the collection of debts by an independent third party or a collection agency. Debt collectors are allowed to contact a debtor:
- In person
- By mail
- By telephone
- By telegram
- By fax

Third party collectors are restricted from contacting debtors at inconvenient times or places. Third party collectors are prohibited from contacting debtors at their place of employment if the agency is aware that the debtor's employer disapproves of this action. Third party collectors are prohibited from certain harassing or abusive practices.

The Fair Debt Collection Practices Act (FDCPA), is a United States statute added in 1978 as part of the Consumer Credit Protection Act. Its purposes are to eliminate abusive practices in the collection of consumer debts, to promote fair debt collection and to provide consumers with an avenue for disputing and obtaining validation of debt information in order to ensure the information's accuracy. The Act creates guidelines under which debt collectors may conduct business, defines rights of consumers involved with debt collectors, and prescribes penalties and remedies for violations of the Act. It is sometimes used in conjunction with the Fair Credit Reporting Act.

Consumer debts are regulated by the FDCPA. The FDCPA defines a consumer debt as "any obligation or alleged obligation of a consumer to pay money arising out of a transaction in which the money, property, insurance, or services which are the subject of the transaction are primarily for personal, family, or household purposes, whether or not such obligation has been reduced to judgment." This can include purchases of an automobile, for medical care, or any charge account.

REMEMBER: Business debts are not regulated by the FDCPA. Although the FDCPA offers some protections, it only applies under certain circumstances:

The debt must be a consumer debt
The collector cannot be the original creditor.

The Federal Trade Commission has the authority to administratively enforce the FDCPA using its powers under the Federal Trade Commission Act. Annoyed consumers may also file a private lawsuit in a state or federal court to collect damages (actual, statutory, attorney's fee and court-costs) from third-party debt collectors. The FDCPA is a strict liability law, which means that a consumer need not prove actual damages in order to claim statutory damages of up to $1,000 plus reasonable attorney fees if a debt collector is proven to have violated the FDCPA. The collector may, however, escape penalty if it shows that the violation (or violations) was the result of a "bona fide error."

Alternately, if the consumer loses the lawsuit and the court determines that the consumer filed the case in bad faith and for the purposes of harassment, the court may then award attorney's fees to the debt collector.

The Federal Trade Commission's Fair Debt Collection Practices Act enforcement begins with investigations of debt collectors identified through complaints. If an investigation reveals a

FDCPA violation, the FTC may proceed with their own attorneys by filing suit in Federal court or the FTC may request that the Department of Justice file suit in Federal court on behalf of the FTC.

The Act prohibits certain types of "abusive and deceptive" conduct when attempting to collect debts, including the following:

Hours for phone contact: contacting consumers by telephone outside of the hours of 8:00 a.m. to 9:00 p.m. local time.

Contact after being asked to stop: contacting consumers in any way (other than litigation) after receiving *written* notice that the consumer wishes no further contact or refuses to pay the alleged debt, with certain exceptions, including advising that collection efforts are being terminated or that the collector intends to file a lawsuit or pursue other remedies where permitted

Contacting consumers at their place of employment after having been told verbally or in writing that this is not acceptable

Contacting consumer known to be represented by an attorney

Contacting consumer after request for validation: contacting the consumer or pursuing collection efforts by the debt collector *after* receipt of a consumer's written request for verification of a debt (or for the name and address of the original creditor on a debt) and *before* the debt collector mails the consumer the requested verification or original creditor's name and address

Misrepresentation or deceit: misrepresenting the debt or using deception to collect the debt, including a debt collector's misrepresentation that he or she is an attorney or law enforcement officer

Publishing the consumer's name or address on a "bad debt" list

Seeking unjustified amounts, which would include demanding any amounts not permitted under an applicable contract or as provided under applicable law

Threatening arrest or legal action that is either not permitted or not actually contemplated

Abusive or profane language used in the course of communication related to the debt

Contact with third parties: revealing or discussing the nature of debts with third parties *(other than the consumer's spouse or attorney)* or threatening such action

Contact by embarrassing media, such as communicating with a consumer regarding a debt by post card, or using any language or symbol, other than the debt collector's address, on any envelope when communicating with a consumer by use of postal mail or by telegram, except that a debt collector may use his business name if such name does not indicate that he is in the debt collection business

Reporting false information on a consumer's credit report or threatening to do so in the process of collection

According to the Federal Trade Commission the most frequent complaint against debt collectors is that they attempted to collect debts that consumers did not owe or a debt where the amount due had been inflated. Another frequent complaint is that the collectors harassed consumers by calling them repeatedly or continuously. In 2007, 19.7% (or 13,989) of FDCPA complaints were for:

Obscene, profane and/or abusive language

Calling during off hours (1,402 complaints)

Using or threatening violence if they did not pay (219 consumers)

Falsely threatening legal action (4,592 consumers)

Improper 3rd party contacts

Failure to send written notice of a debt

Failure to state who the debt is owed to

Failure to provide instruction on disputing the debt & requesting verification

Failure to verify debts

Continuing to contact debtors after receiving cease & desist letters

Some examples of things that collectors have done that are unfair practices according to the act:

Attempting to collect more money than was due under the contract.
Asking for, accepting, depositing or threatening to deposit a post dated check.
Making collect calls
Using post cards in collection efforts
Writing "Dead beat" on the outside of an envelope sent to the debtor.
Threatening to or actually repossessing personal property of the debtor.
Trying to collect on a debt that is past the statute of limitations.
Some examples of harassment and abuse are:
Threatening to use violence to collect the debt.
Using obscene, profane or abusive language or embarrassing the debtor.

Calling endlessly and repeatedly.
Calling without identifying yourself.
Calling a debtor when they know they are represented by an attorney.
Contacting the customer after receiving a cease & desist letter.
Discussing the debt with third parties.
Using letters that appear to look like legal documents.

What Debt collectors cannot do:
Collectors cannot talk about debts to third parties.
Collectors can only contact a third party once in an effort to locate a debtor.
Collectors cannot use postcards.
Collectors cannot put "collection language" on the outside of an envelope.
Collectors cannot communicate with a debtor who has an attorney.
Collectors cannot call a debtor before 8 a.m. or after 9 p.m. in their time zone.
Collectors cannot call a debtor at work if the employer prohibits it.
Collectors cannot harass, oppress or abuse a debtor.
Collectors cannot threaten violence.
Collectors cannot swear or use abusive language.
Collectors cannot "publish" names of debtors.
Collectors cannot call a debtor repeatedly.
Collectors cannot call a debtor and then not identify themselves.
Collectors cannot use false or misleading representations.
Collectors cannot claim they are affiliated with a government agency.
Collectors cannot misrepresent the amount or legal status of the debt.
Collectors cannot claim they are attorneys.
Collectors cannot threaten a debtor with arrest, prison, repossession, or attachment if they don't' intend to take those actions and state law permits it.
Collectors cannot threaten legal action if they don't intend to legally take it.
Collectors cannot falsely tell a debtor that they have committed a crime.
Collectors cannot make false reports to the credit reports of debtors.
Collectors cannot use any false or deceptive actions in the collection of debts.
Collectors cannot use fake company names.

The FTC recognizes that third party debt collectors contact millions of consumers each year. The number of consumer complaints the FTC receives about these collectors is only a small percentage of the overall number of consumers contacted.

The "Fair Housing Act" makes it illegal for lenders to discriminate in housing related lending. There protections apply to the applicant and to anyone who might lease, rent or occupy a home. The "Equal Credit Opportunity Act" applies to all type of lending and prohibits discrimination on the basis of sex, race, color, religion, national original, marital status, age or if you may be receiving state of public assistance.

The "Truth in Lending Act" gives you the right to be given details such as how much the loan is going to cost, what the payments will be and when they are due, BEFORE you sign any loan agreement.

The "Equal Credit Opportunity Act" sets requirements when you submit an application for a loan. A lender must act on your application within 30 days. If you are denied the loan, the lender is required by law to send you a notice outlining the reasons for the denial, if you request it.

The "Fair Credit Billing Act" protects you if there is an error made on your bill by any lender. You must submit a dispute in writing within 60 days.

The "Fair Debt Collection Practices Act" protects consumers if they have been placed for collection. You should become familiar with this act if you have accounts in collections; this act protects you from misleading or abusive collection practices.

Important things to know

Collectors can still sue you if you are making payments they do not feel are significant enough in relation to the debt amount. (This would be if you owed $10,000.00 for example and were sending $5 a month, that doesn't even cover the interest)

Recording phone conversations without the consent of the other party is legal in some states.

Collectors can't call you before 8am in your time zone and after 9pm.

Collectors can't call you at work if your employer forbids it.

Collectors can call your neighbors, family and friends to find you, they just can't tell them it is because you owe money.

Once you have an attorney, a collector can only deal with the attorney. If they call you, contact the attorney and file a complaint.

Collectors cannot use threats of violence, profanity or any false statements, repeated use of a telephone to annoy or harass or give false credit information about a debtor to anyone.

Remember you cannot be put in jail for failure to pay a debt, if a collector tells you this hang up and file a complaint.

Resources

To file a complaint against a collector or creditor's in-house collector call: (877)FTC-HELP or visit www.FTC.gov to email them

The FTC also has free publications and videos about dealing with debt and collectors at www.ftc.gov/credit, some of these publications are:

Debt Collection FAQ's: A Guide for Consumers
Need a Lawyer? Judge for yourself.
Dealing with debt collectors (Video)

You can write to them at:
Federal Trade Commission
600 Pennsylvania, NW, H-130
Washington, DC 20580
(877) 382-4357

File a complaint with your state consumer protection agency through the National Association of Attorney Generals http://www.naag.org/

Find a reputable accredited debt counseling agency
National Foundation for Credit Counseling   http://www.nfcc.org/
Association of Independent Consumer Credit Counseling Agencies   http://www.aiccca.org/

The National consumer Law Center   http://www.nclc.org/

U.S. Department of Housing and Urban Development 1-800-669-9777

Debtors Anonymous http://www.debtorsanonymous.org/

Sample Dispute Letter

Date
Your name
Your address
City, state, zip code

Company name
Address
City, state, zip code

Re: **Any reference or account number you may have goes here**

To whom it may concern,

I am writing to dispute the following information found on the attached copy of my credit report.

(Identify the item) **The credit card account** is inaccurate **or disputed or incomplete** because (describe why it is disputed) I paid the collection agency on June 4th 2007.

Enclosed are copies of (send copies of any documentation to support your dispute) of my check dated June 4th, 2007 and the back where it was deposited into your account.

Please investigate this important matter and correct this item as soon as possible.

Sincerely,
Your name

Enclosures: (list any copies you are enclosing) Copy of check front
                                          Copy of check back
                                          Copy of bank statement

Monthly Budget Worksheet

Monthly Budget Worksheet

Expenses	Monthly Bill
HOME	
Mortgage/Rent	$ _____
Taxes & Insurance	$ _____
Repairs	$ _____
UTILITIES	
Electric	$ _____
Fuel	$ _____
Water & Sewer	$ _____
Phone	$ _____
Cell Phone	$ _____
Cable	$ _____
Internet	$ _____
TRANSPORTATION	
Car Payment	$ _____
Fuel	$ _____
Insurance	$ _____
Repairs/Maintenance	$ _____
Tolls, parking	$ _____
INSURANCE	
Life insurance	$ _____
Health insurance	$ _____
FOOD	
Groceries	$ _____
Eating out	$ _____
FAMILY EXPENSES	
Day Care	$ _____
Child Support	$ _____
School	$ _____
PERSONAL	
Hair/nails	$ _____
Medication	$ _____
Toiletries/Make up	$ _____
Clothes	$ _____

LOANS/CREDIT CARDS
Credit Cards $ _____
(Minimum payments) $ _____
                             $ _____
Loans $ _____

PETS
Food $ _____
Vet $ _____
Grooming, care $ _____

FUN!
Books, newspapers
Magazines $ _____
Movies $ _____
Bowling, golf $ _____
Anything else $ _____

TOTAL MONTHLY BILLS $ _____

YOUR MONTHLY EARNINGS $ _____

Your earnings minus your monthly bills = $ _____

Are you looking at a negative number? Go back and cut back on some expenses. If something seems too hard to give up, give it up for one month and try it. Debt is stressful, adjusting to a budget can be tough work in the beginning but the rewards are great.

Fix your Credit

Order free copies of your credit reports every year. To get a free copy of your credit reports, visit www.AnnualCreditReport.com   There you can request free credit reports, **online**, by **phone** or through the **mail**.

ONLINE   Free credit reports requested online are viewable immediately upon authentication of identity.

PHONE   Free credit reports requested by phone or mail will be processed within 15 days or receipt. To request your credit reports by phone call 1-877-322-8228

MAIL   To request your credit reports by mail visit https://www.annualcreditreport.com/cra/requestformfinal.pdf

Print out the form, fill it out and mail to:
Annual Credit Report Request Service
P.O. Box 105281
Atlanta, GA 30348-5281

Your reports will be mailed to you within 15 days. allow 2-3 weeks for delivery.

The (FCRA) Fair Credit Reporting Act, requires each of the 3 credit bureaus to provide you with a free copy of your credit report annually at your request. Don't ask each credit bureau for your report, visit annualcreditreport.com, a website set up just for this purpose. Also, if you are denied credit or employment because of your credit, you can request a free copy of your credit report.

Next take these 6 steps to clean up your reports:

Step 1: Order the copies of your credit reports. For free from all three credit bureaus once a year by visiting www.annualcreditreport.com or calling toll free 877-322-8228. This way you can see what is on your report and what your credit score is, and then you can take steps to improve it. Anyone who is in this situation should do this TODAY to begin the process.

Step 2: Make sure everything on your report is legitimate, if you don't agree with something on your report, send a letter to the credit bureaus disputing the item and explaining why and ask that it be attached to your credit report until the item is removed. Credit bureaus are required to do this and when someone pulls your report they are obligated by law to disregard that item. If you ask, the consumer reporting company must send notices to anyone who received your report within the last 6 months AND you can have a corrected copy of your report sent to anyone who received a copy during the last 2 years for employment purposes.

Step 3: Cancel any credit accounts still listed as open accounts on your report, this will show the account was cancelled by the consumer, boosting your credit rating.

Step 4: When you call your credit card companies to cancel the cards, tell them you are trying to pay off your balance and ask if they can waive any late fees or over the limit charges, this will lower your bill as soon as the credit is issued. Many credit card companies will do this, but you must cancel the card.

Step 5: Make all payments on time, even if it is just a minimum payment, do this for 3 months and you will see your credit rating start improving, the longer you do this, the better your rating becomes. Pay off higher balances with higher interest rates first or smaller balances that you can pay off in 1 or 2 payments to bring to a zero balance quickly.

Step 6: If your situation is serious, contact a legitimate non-profit credit counseling service, avoid any company that promises you a quick reversal of your credit problems, they are a scam and you will be wasting your money.

How do you improve your credit score?

- Pay your bills on time – this will raise your score.
- Keep credit card balances low – carrying high balances of debt can lower your score.
- Pay off as much debt as you can.
- Don't apply for credit often, each time you apply for credit somewhere and someone pulls your credit report, that lowers your score.

How do you dispute an item on your credit report?

Make sure everything on your report is correct. If you don't agree with something send them a letter disputing the item and explain why you are disputing the item and ask that while you are disputing this item, your letter be attached to your credit report. Make sure to include copies of any documentation that supports your claim. Send the letter by certified mail with return receipt requested and keep copies of everything you send. Also send a copy to the creditor who reported the information. This way when a potential employer pulls your report they will be obligated to disregard that item. If something is corrected or removed from your report you are entitled to another free copy of your report.

How can I increase my income to pay more on my debts?

When I was getting divorced I ran into a bad situation and turned to a credit counseling service that was a scam and I spent money I didn't have that never went towards any of my debt. Be very careful of credit counseling services, make sure they are non-profit and check all of their references, including the better business bureau. Talk to some of their customers and make sure they are legitimate.

Some of the things I did to increase my income were to cancel many things I had but that weren't necessities. For example, cancel cable television, cancel cell phones if you won't be charged an early termination fee, or cut back on all the bells and whistles such as call waiting, call forwarding, caller ID or anything you can live without, and we can all live without a lot more than we think.

Use coupons at the grocery store, carpool to work, stop going out to eat and bring lunch and coffee from home to your job. Don't renew magazine subscriptions, utilize your library for books, magazines and even the internet.

A great way to see how much you will add to your income is to try this simple exercise, just do this for one month and you will truly be amazed at how much money you spend on little things here and there. For example, I used a small notebook and kept it in my bag, write the date at the top of the page and every time you buy something, write it down. I did this and wrote down when I bought a coffee, newspaper, magazine, candy bar, gum, gas, extra minutes on your cell phone.

You will really be AMAZED at how much this all adds up to, I am a frugal person and my extras added up to what I could make at a part time job! Now once you do this, don't start spending that money on anything but your debt, use it to pay off any bills you have and you will improve your credit and your state of mind tremendously. So to review what you have learned so far, here are some tips on staying out of debt, how to avoid getting into more debt and what three things you can do today to change your situation.

How can I stay out of debt?

- Don't use Credit cards, use your debit card, that way you are using only money you have.
- Pay with cash or your debit card whenever possible.
- Live within your means.
- Avoid "buy now, pay later" types of offers.
- Cut back on something in your budget to increase your income.
- Save money for things you want to buy instead of buying it on credit.
- Keep a budget, and change it when you need to but always follow a budget.

Tips to avoid falling into debt are:

- Cut up all credit cards, use your debt card, this way you are only using money you have.
- Pay with cash or your debit card whenever possible.
- Live within your means.
- Avoid "buy now, pay later" and "interest-free financing" offers.
- Cut down on unnecessary expenses, such as cell phones, cable television, Starbucks, magazine subscriptions and try to carpool to work.
- Save for anything you want to buy rather than paying for it with credit.
- Start a budget and stick to it! Consider it a challenge and be strong and you will win!

Top 3 things you can do right now to feel better about your situation.

1. Start a budget, use the worksheet included in this report.
2. Contact your creditors; tell them you lost your job, or whatever the case may be. Tell them you are having trouble making the payments. Ask to modify your payments; this is MUCH better than doing nothing and having the account turned over to a collection agency.
3. Credit counseling might be for you. If you don't know where to begin and really feel as though you need the help of a professional, seek credit counseling. Be skeptical of businesses that offer instant solutions to credit problems.

Michelle Dunn is a 24 year debt collection industry veteran, entrepreneur, award winning author, self-syndicated columnist, one of the Top 5 Women in Collections and one of the Top 50 most influential collection professionals in her industry. She has been a debtor and a collector, look for her books on Kindle and in bookstores everywhere.

Now available for Kindle!

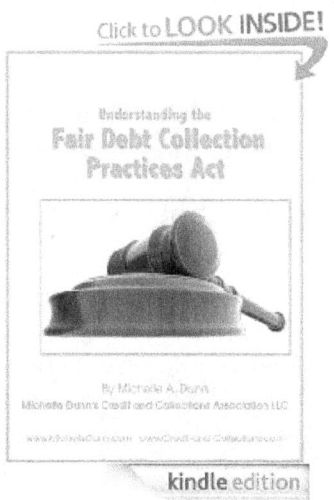

Learn more at www.Credit-and-Collections.com & ww.MichelleDunn.com

Michelle Dunn

If you found this book helpful, please leave a review on amazon.com so others can know that this book helped you and can help them. Thank you for buying and reading my book, it was hard to write my personal story and I hope that by sharing my story, I have helped you. – *Michelle Dunn*

To post a review visit: http://www.amazon.com/Dealing-Aggressive-Collectors-industry-ebook/dp/B007B2AQO0/

Thank you very much!